DREAMS COME TRUE

Other STELLA NOTES BOOKS

- ❖ Law of Attraction
- ❖ Imagine
- ❖ Dreams Come True
- ❖ Being Happier
- ❖ Inspired
- ❖ No Worries
- ❖ Happy by Habit
- ❖ The Power of No
- ❖ Stuck No More
- ❖ Love Thyself
- ❖ Mindfully Yours
- ❖ Find Your Purpose

Every Month we add new titles in our Happiness Library filled with tips and tools to make your journey a Fun One! Be sure to check them out!

♥♥♥

Praise For Stella's Coaching Program "The Ticket"

I first met Stella at a meeting for business professionals. She had a fifty-thousand-watt smile that made me wish for my sunglasses. I avoided her. Slowly, I began to see the authenticity behind the smile and her sincere intention to facilitate people's lives becoming richer and more fulfilled.

When the opportunity to participate in her program presented itself I was in. Her programs are demanding, requiring plenty of action and introspection in return there are a cornucopia of rewards.

Gaining clarity, focus and direction as well as having her formidable ability to support each person's transformation has been priceless. It surprised me how beneficial being a part of a group has been. The folks in each of her programs became a valuable tool for holding myself accountable to complete the goals I set for myself each week.

Their success and newly enlightened awareness became as much a reason to celebrate as my own. Plus, when I would momentarily lose my way they were there, right along with Stella, holding the space and belief I would succeed.

I am grateful to have said yes to her programs of accelerated growth and progress. Oh and I often find myself with a big grin on my face.

Thank you Stella!

Nancy Westphal, Diplomat Certified Craniosacral Therapist, mentored by Dr. John Upledger, DO, OMM

Praise For Stella's "Steps to Success" Corporate Training and "Stella Notes"

Stella is definitely the "Queen of Happiness" and her passion to make this world a happier place is an art form, that Leonardo da Vinci would be proud of.

I have seen Stella speak with various audiences, and she has captivated their attention for many hours at a time. Stella speaks from the heart and soul, and her words are very inspirational in helping people back on the road to true happiness in a simple and spiritual way.

Her **Stella Notes** *series of books gives even the "no time to read" individuals, the ability to change their lives in a positive way that will bring true happiness even in times of despair. To know Stella is to love everything about her, and she will touch your heart with Solutions from the Soul that will make your life a better and happier one!*

John Ondrejack, P.E.
Manager-Southeast/Caribbean Region
Water Resource/Power Pump Sales
Flowserve Solutions Group

Praise For Stella's Corporate Training "Steps to Success"

I had the pleasure of booking Stella Frances to conduct a workshop for my Alumni Group at Unity Behavioral Health, located in Hobe Sound, Florida. The participants included newly sober young men and women who had recently discharged from our addiction treatment program. As you can imagine, there are many obstacles including fear and depression- as well as anxiety at coming back into a culture and experience with new tools and ideas.

Stella's course / workshop was exactly what my group needed to help shift their mindset into one of hope, faith and happiness! It was interactive and played upon many of the topics that they learned while in treatment including, self-esteem, self-discipline, goals, and having FUN! Stella's wonderful energy and beautiful spirit shined through enabling the group to connect with her and really hear her message of self and happiness!

I would definitely have her back for a second round!

Sincerely,

Stephany Mathews, Alumni Services,
Unity Behavioral Health

DREAMS COME TRUE

Creating A Wonderful Life

STELLA FRANCES

Happiness Coach & Success Trainer

Alpha ★ Aster Press

Copyright © 2019 by Stella Frances

All rights reserved. Printed in the United States of America.
This book or any portion thereof may not be reproduced or used in any manner whatsoever without the express written permission of the publisher except for the use of brief quotations in critical articles and reviews.
For information address: Alpha Aster Press, 103 S Us Hwy One, Ste F-5, Jupiter, FL, 33477

First Printing: 2019

ISBN 978-0-359-53575-0

Alpha★Aster Press

Cover design: ZettaKarmas.com
Photos of Stella: WoodstockStudio.com
Other photos: Source Internet, Pixabay.com

Ordering Information: Special discounts are available on quantity purchases by corporations, associations, educators, and others. For details, contact the publisher at the above listed address.

U.S. trade bookstores and wholesalers, contact Alpha★Aster Press
sales@alphaaster.com

This book is dedicated to You:

Wishing you the best of success in discovering your dream. I know you can make it come true, if you believe in you.

I Believe In You.

Stella Frances

---

*Very little is needed to make a happy life;
it is all within yourself, in your way of thinking.*
MARCUS AURELIUS

CONTENTS

Preface iii
Introduction by Stella Frances vii

ACT I: INFORMATIVE GUIDEBOOK 1

    Introduction 3

    « Chapter One » Be Open To Your Dream 5

    « Chapter Two » Follow Your Dream 11

    « Chapter Three » Make Your Dream Come True 21

ACT II: EMPOWERING WORKBOOK 29

    « Chapter Four » Take Action Toward Your Dream 31

ACT III: KEY FACTS 45

    « Chapter Five » Discover Your Passion 47

    Notes At A Glance 61

ACT IV: TOOLS-TO-USE 67

    « Chapter Six » Happiness Builders 69

        Words Of Wisdom 72

        Pearls Of Kindness 76

        Relaxing Mandalas 79

IN CLOSING: Bonus Material - A Gift For You 85

AFTERWORD: Resource Guide For Living Happier Life 89

Acknowledgments

I acknowledge with heartfelt happiness and gratitude:

My clients and students for their encouragement to spread the word about true happiness through the Stella Notes.

My participants to my seminars and presentations who have shown their support for my work and who continue to be an inspiration to me.

My mentors and teachers who shared their knowledge and wisdom with me, while they believed in my wildest dream and breakthrough goal: To spread happiness around the globe!

Everyone who makes the effort to bring a smile to the world, even on the days the sun's hiding behind the clouds.

My awesome friends, amazing family, and the best sister in the whole wide world who surround me with unconditional love, smiles, and fun times.

Knowing yourself is the beginning of all wisdom.
ARISTOTLE

"I believe we were born to be happy"
Mentor, Coach, Speaker, Creator of Stella-Notes

Hi and thank you for checking out this publication. Stella Frances, here, founder of Elevated Awareness, on a mission to empower you.

My goal is to add more value to your world than you ever thought possible by giving you tools you can use to live a great life.

Having trained with Jack Canfield, America's #1 Success Coach and Co-Author of "Chicken Soup for the Soul", and as a certified DreamBuilder Coach, I am known to deliver innovative and high-quality personal development training with proven results that have changed many lives.

I help people like you dream big and back it up with daily actions to create measurable results. That's because I care deeply about you and I am committed to not only get you results but make learning irresistibly fun.

Through my products, seminars, and programs you'll learn practical wisdom and how to apply it to your everyday life. Through the Stella Notes, I want to encourage you and inspire you to take charge of your happiness and success by boosting your life and business skills, dropping excuses and adding massive amounts of fun into your every day.

Make the most of the Stella Notes by completing the exercises, practicing daily affirmation, and building new habits that will contribute to taking your happiness and wellbeing to the next level. Much Love, Stella Frances

THE GREATEST GIFT: YOUR OWN PERSONAL DEVELOPMENT

The Stella Notes is all about personal development for everyone, within the context of self-discovery & transformation. Personal development is the ongoing, lifelong process of learning, knowing and understanding who we are, why we're here and what work we have come to do in our lifetime, what our gifts and abilities are, and how to build them up, so that we can live up to our highest potential.

If you find yourself in a situation that needs to change. If you have reached a plateau wondering what's next, look at the "man/woman in the mirror" and decide to make a change by changing your ways. the *Stella Notes* gives you winning ways to successfully do so.

CLUB ★ HAPPY

Know thyself.
SOCRATES

The success that followed the launching of the Stella Notes led me to the next step which was to create a loving, caring, physical or virtual space, where we get to connect, share ideas, and support each other. And so, the Club was born!

"Club-Happy" is not your ordinary book club. Consider it your social group, your support group, your mastermind group, your cheerleader group. Once a week we get together in-person or on a call to connect by brainstorming new ideas, solving problems, learning from each other and growing together.

Fact of life is that we need each other to grow and evolve, especially when we decide to make a change. Our motto at the Club-Happy is simple. We come together with the aim to live better lives by finding and implementing empowering solutions to the problems we are experiencing in our personal and professional lives. The intention of Club-Happy is to help each other grow and expand by implementing the practices, tools, and strategies that are included in the Stella Notes books.

Be Part Of An Empowering Group Of People

Having 2,000 friends on Facebook may be great but personal connections are much more powerful. Club-Happy is about building great relationships personal and professional, as we get together and connect by sharing knowledge and helping each other grow.

As a member of Club-Happy you are an important part of a conscious community that shares the same vision. The vision of attaining and maintaining true happiness. A peaceful, balanced, and harmonious way of being.

There are so many reasons why join Club-Happy. Every in-person meeting or call is well structured with clear boundaries and expectations, runs based on a mutually agreed upon agenda to help us stay on track as we share evenly.

Why Join CLUB★HAPPY:

1. To create deep, lasting connections with like-minded people.
2. To clear confusion and gain focus and clarity on your vision.
3. To be courageous, advantageous and spontaneous.
4. To become the person, you know you can be.
5. To create a clear vision and an action plan.
6. To socialize and be part of a fun group.
7. To think bigger and more creatively.
8. To be accountable.
9. To support others.
10. To be supported.
11. To be happier.
12. To be You.

I invite you to join me today and start enjoying the tremendous benefits of being part of Club-Happy. Visit https://stellafrances.com/clubhappy/ for more information or reach out with your questions, at Happier@StellaFrances.com

INTRODUCTION BY STELLA FRANCES
Suggestions To My Readers

A very warm welcome to this reading experience. My intention for creating the Stella Notes, series of practical books, is very specific. I want to help you harness your inner-power, connect with your truth, and create a life that is in harmony with your soul. And in return I promise, you will get to deep lasting happiness, for the only place to find your true happy is within you.

The Stella Notes will help you learn new ways of bringing positive change into your life in the most effective winning ways with the least amount of effort. Originally, I created the *Stella Notes,* with a specific audience in the mind of my heart. The people who have no time to read and the people who are not fans of reading. **My sister gave me the idea.** Knowledge is power, but reading is not her favorite past time.

As an artist, my sister Zetta, loves to paint. Often, I'd hear her say, *"If there was a book for non-readers, I would read it."* By that she meant, a few pages, clear language easy to read, helpful to the point useful material and of course pictures. Being an avid reader myself I didn't want her to miss out on knowledge and so here we are.

How To Use The Stella Notes Books

The Stella Notes is a series of books structured to make reading and absorption of the material real easy. The information is presented in four sections. Each section is called **ACT**. Here's what you will find in every Stella Notes book:

- ❖ **ACT I:** Guidebook: Theory of Concept.
- ❖ **ACT II:** Workbook: Self-Reflection on the Concept.
- ❖ **ACT III:** Key Facts: Additional Information.
- ❖ **ACT IV:** Mindful and Practical Tools-to-Use.

You can read the guidebook in *ACT I* at one seating or in small bits, however it suits you. Answer the questions in the workbook as presented in *ACT II* at your pace. Here, you can write down the answers in your book or get a notebook and start jotting them down there. In *ACT III* **Key Facts** you will find additional information about the main subject.

While in *ACT IV* you will be pleasantly surprised by a beautiful collection of words of wisdom, pearls of kindness in the form of heartfelt affirmations, and magnificent mandalas to help you stay in the moment, find inner peace and express your inner-artist. The pearls of kindness are beautiful positive statements designed to help you build new empowering beliefs through repetition. The words of wisdom I bring to you, were spoken by some of the most powerful and advanced thinkers in our world. Listen to the echo of their voices and use their valuable knowledge in your moment-to-moment life.

In the Afterword section, under resources you will find tools you can use to build the above ideas and they are all totally **FREE**. This is my way of saying Thank You. *Go to the website StellaFrances.com/resources and download them there.* Use the *Gratitude Journal* to record you wins and gifts of the day. Use the *Get Unstuck Tool* for days when you feel just a tad stuck…we all go there and need this tool. Same with the *Priority Finder Tool.*

Who doesn't get stressed or overwhelmed with the complexities of our lives? The *Daily Success Habits* will help you with just that. Create new success habits. Finally, the *5-Day Grow-Expand-Thrive Mini Course* will help you exhilarate towards your new life. The life of your choice.

Why Read The Stella Notes Books? Because You Will Learn New, Winning Ways Of Thinking...Guarantee!

The practice of planting high quality seedlings of new positive, powerful, constructive thoughts in our minds creates our ideal results. I've been practicing and experimenting this truth for the past 20 years. I know it works.

Remember this. To change your LifeStyle, you must first change your ThoughtStyle. Opening up to the thoughts of great thinkers is one sure way to get inspired and start thinking different thoughts. Makes sense? Albert Einstein defined insanity as the act of trying to solve a problem with the same thinking that created it.

At first, it may seem or even feel a little strange but stay with it. Give it time, let it flourish. You will be amazed at what you will harvest.

Happiness is the meaning and the purpose of life, the whole aim and end of human existence.
ARISTOTLE

Are You Willing To Believe In Yourself?

Finally, a word of caution. As with anything worth having in life it takes time, commitment and dedication. It takes effort to create something worth having.

❖ *What's worth more than, living a life you totally love living?*

❖ *What's worth more than, being happy from within?*

❖ *What's worth more than, having found meaning in your life?*

So, go ahead dare to design your life, find meaning and live it the way you want, for you know best how to find what you're looking for. And as you do, practice self-love through kindness and forgiveness towards yourself. Be patient with you.

Be the light of love in your life. Give yourself the best love you can give yourself. **<u>BELIEVE IN YOU</u>. And when you do, you will be amazed as you discover who you truly are and what you can create when you release the brakes of yesterday.**

Read the Stella Notes, Solutions from the Soul, any way you like. Cover to cover, one paragraph, one quote, one affirmation at a time. Keep your book by your side, make it your constant companion. It is designed in such way that however you use it you will feel inspired to move forward from where you are.

Whether you read one page, one sentence or just run the questions you will start seeing changes and eventually results in your life. You will find yourself be more motivated, more engaged, more curious, more alive and above all happier.

"Magically?" You may ask.

Well, life is magical and so are you. Once you start tapping into your super powers there will be no stopping. You have in your procession an amazing tool, an extraordinary component. That is your brain. And you are given unlimited potential. Put them to work with the information I will be sharing with you through the Stella Notes books and you will be well on your way to creating pure and lasting happiness and unstoppably so.

You are brave. Choose to leave behind the voice of fear and doubt and you will be amazed at what you will create. Courage is not the absence of fear. Courage is facing fear.

The Stella Notes books bring you unique concepts that focus on mindset, contribute to your personal growth, and provide you with tools you can use and strategies to implement that will help you change your thoughts and therefore your world.

Let's begin!

With Love and Gratitude,
XO Stella

P.S. If you know it's time to bring radical change into your life and need support, reach out and contact me through the website. I am here to help.

ACT I:

INFORMATIVE GUIDEBOOK

knowledge:
the pathway to happiness
& success

The future belongs to those who believe in the beauty of their dreams.
-Eleanor Roosevelt

Dreams Come True
Creating A Wonderful Life

Introduction

"Dream as if you'll live forever. Live as if you'll die today." ~ James Dean

Your life is a wonderful gift. Each day, you can do anything you want, any way you want, any time you want. You might be saying to yourself, "I seem to be caught in the humdrum of my life right now" or "I'm struggling to achieve my life goals. How can I get to a place where I can do whatever I want?"

The fact is that you're choosing everything that's happening now, even though you may feel stuck in your current life situation.

If you can imagine what you really want and allow your dreams to come to the surface of your mind, you can do great things. You have the power to achieve the life you've always wanted, simply by opening your mind to the dreams you may have been afraid to dream in the past.

This book brings you wisdom that can change your life. The wise words, shown in the form of quotes, expressed by some of the most advanced thinkers of all times carry tremendous value and potency and can help you create the incredible life that you aspire to live.

Study each quote, reflect on the discussion, and then put the tips for each quote into action. The quotations can be interpreted in many ways, so feel free to put your own spin on it. What does each quote mean to you?

Get ready.

Your dream life is waiting for you to go after it.

« Chapter One »

BE OPEN TO YOUR DREAM

"All human beings are also dream beings. Dreaming ties all mankind together." ~Jack Kerouac

KEROUAC BELIEVED that having life dreams is a given for each of us. And because all humans dream, we're then connected to one another by the thread of having our own desires.

The occurrence of our dreams then is an intimate way that we can understand each other because we're all engaging in the same type of thinking and imagining of what we can achieve in life.

How far can you go in imagining whatever you want in life?

It's comforting to know that we all share the promise of dreaming up the existence we want.

Consider these suggestions to be open to your dreams:

Tap into what truly matters to you. Maybe your dream is to run your own business, travel the world, or own a piece of land with a modest home. Ponder your greatest wishes.

Make your life be an illustration of your fondest hopes. The best wish you can have for yourself is that in your daily existence, you show yourself and others what your dreams are. In simplistic terms, live your dreams.

Encourage yourself to ponder your dreams daily. Think about the specifics of your life's dreams sometime during your day, regardless of how busy you are. You can even do so at the same time several days a week. For example, if you get a fifteen-minute break at work in the morning, you could use that quarter-hour to think about your dreams.

Recognize that it's human to have wishes and hopes. It's never silly or childish to have dreams. As Kerouac has said, all humankind possesses their wishes and hopes for what they want their lives to be. The same goes for you.

Share your truest dreams out loud with someone. Hearing yourself speak about your dreams is inspiring and helps to clarify the goals you truly wish to pursue. Try it.

We're all in this life together, dreaming our own personal magic within. The sooner you accept this concept, the easier it will be for you to allow yourself to be more forthcoming and open with yourself and others about what you yearn for.

Choose Your Dream

"You can plant a dream."
~Anne Campbell

This short, simple saying packs a pretty big punch. One interpretation is that, regardless of where you are in life, you can illustrate your own picture of what you'd like your life to be like. The quote implies that a dream doesn't just come to you randomly. You can decide what your dream will be.

Plant your own dream by taking these three steps:

Make a decision about where you want to live. A huge part of cultivating your own dream is being in the place where you can make it happen.

Ask if you're in the job that you would choose now for yourself. What you spend your time doing each day is an important aspect of your life. Ensure that it's fascinating and wonderful to you.

Do what you love to do. What activities bring out your passion? Do you make time to do some of them each day? Planting your own dream means that you'll allow yourself the time and opportunity to go after that which delivers anticipation, joy, and interest to you.

Feed and water your dream. Arrange your life around what you want. Only then can you get past the planting stage. For example, perhaps you dream of becoming a golf pro, but the nearest golf course is 20 miles away. What could you do to make it easier for you to golf more often?

Planting your dream can be scary, exciting, and invigorating. It might also take some time and planning. However, when you acknowledge your own hopes, you're one step closer to achieving and living them.

Nix the Naysayers

"He was a dreamer, a thinker, a speculative philosopher...or, as his wife would have it, an idiot." ~Douglas Adams

This quote brings humor to the whole idea of dreaming, yet encases a powerful point. Regardless of what you can think or dream up, there will always be someone who attempts to put a damper on it.

Ponder these suggestions about how to dream your biggest dreams, regardless of the naysayers:

Develop your own philosophies. When you let yourself consider what could be, you're building a thought-by-thought philosophy of your own.

Accept the fact that there may be others who disagree with your ideas. Use their negativity to spur you forward to accomplish your goals.

List the subjects that you find yourself thinking about. Look for recurrent themes. For example, maybe you find yourself disagreeing with the politics that your co-workers often espouse. Although you can avoid opening up to them about your disagreement if that's your choice, you can at least identify subjects that hold great importance to you.

What do you think are the most important aspects of life? Have ideas and opinions about things, especially things that matter personally. Dream. Think. Speculate.

Refuse to allow anyone to deter you. Regardless of what others do or do not believe, carry on with your speculations about what your future can hold. Rather than seek outside reinforcement from others, provide for yourself the impetus you require to move forward in creating your ideal life.

On the way to your dreams, you'll encounter those who are sure that you're crazy for even thinking you could achieve them. Accept the fact that others may not understand the relevance of your dreams to your life, and then dream on anyway.

If you stay the course and remain attached to your dreams, you just might reach your highest heights.

**Your vision
will become clear only when
you look into your heart...
Who looks outside, dreams.
Who looks inside, awakens.**
Carl Jung

« Chapter Two »

FOLLOW YOUR DREAM
Leave Fear Behind and Go After Your Dreams

"All of our dreams can come true if we have the courage to pursue them." ~Walt Disney

THIS ONE SHORT statement sums up well what can happen when we follow our dreams. Walt Disney's story is pretty inspiring, when it comes to truly living your dreams. You're probably familiar with Mr. Disney on some level. He was a famous business entrepreneur and cartoonist, who developed, wrote, produced, and directed his own television shorts, shows, and series, as well as cartoons and films, from 1927 until his death.

Disney was truly a dreamer as he came from humble beginnings in Chicago, rising to become one of the world's most famous Americans. Disney no doubt began dreaming at a young age and continued doing so throughout his life.

Disney's dreams are evident through the multitude of cartoon characters he created, with one of his first-developed characters being Mickey Mouse.

Indeed, because of his dreams, several venues were built around the world to spread his art, joy, and stories: Walt Disney World in Florida, Disneyland in California, Tokyo Disney, Euro Disney, Hong Kong Disneyland, Disney Paris, and Shanghai Disneyland.

The power and promise of dreaming is evident, not only throughout Walt Disney's life, but long after his death in 1966. His brother, Roy, continued to live out Disney's fantasies and plans for the future, and then Walt Disney's surviving children and grandchildren have followed suit upon Roy's death.

The incredible, depth, breadth, and reach into the future of Walt Disney's dreams are true testaments to what can happen if you pursue your dreams.

In his quotation, Disney mentions courage as an integral precursor to bringing dreams to fruition. His statement illustrates that if you have the guts to go after what you want, you can make your dreams happen. The following strategies will help you follow those dreams.

Have courage. Rather than be afraid, jump in with both feet. Be brave enough to set out to accomplish your goals. Expect to feel the anxiety and fear of casting caution to the wind but continue forward anyway.

Create a vision board. As your thoughts and dreams solidify, make a vision board that pictures all the things you dream about. Pick up a piece of poster board from your local discount store. Clip pictures from magazines or the newspaper that relate to your personal vision and glue them to the poster board. Write your comments and draw on it, too.

Take action. Pursue whatever it is you want with a vengeance. Do something each day to move toward your desired goal. For example, read about your interest. Go to your local library and talk to the librarian about how to find information about it.

Consider roadblocks as challenges. Expect to come upon obstacles to your goals. Remind yourself that figuring out how to navigate around the roadblocks will make achieving your goal that much sweeter.

Keep your momentum going. When you believe that all your dreams can come true when you have courage and pursue them, you'll be able to continue ahead with renewed strength and resolve.

Never underestimate your power to make your dreams come true. Think of Walt Disney, his life, and what great things continue to be developed because of his fantasies. If one man can accomplish all of that with his dreams, what can you do with yours?

Hold fast to dreams, for if dreams die, life is a broken-winged bird that cannot fly.
Langston Hughes

Take 100% Responsibility in Bringing Your Dreams to Life

"If you take responsibility for yourself you will develop a hunger to accomplish your dreams." ~Les Brown

This quotation brings up an aspect of dreaming that you may not have considered: responsibility.

Taking responsibility for yourself means that you'll step up to the plate to determine what happens in your life. You become the "point man" for making decisions that serve you best. It's all on you to take action.

An interesting aspect of Brown's quote is that he uses the term, "hunger" to illustrate one's personal drive to create life's dreams. When we're hungry, we go looking for something to eat and we keep seeking sustenance until we find what we want.

Brown believed that when you totally own your life and choices, you'll be driven to accomplish your life goals.

Put the sentiments from this quote into action by answering these questions:

1. Do you take responsibility for your life? To do so, you must avoid blaming others for your choices. When you take responsibility, then you're more likely to do what's necessary to make something work out the way you want.

2. How "hungry" are you? Each day think about your life goals, the ones you truly want to achieve. Do you feel totally driven to go after what you desire? If not, why not?

3. Perhaps the goals you've set for yourself are not the things you really want to achieve. If that's the case, you can take time now to determine what your real dreams are. You can alter your path to ensure you're heading toward your desired life.

4. Are you answering your urges each day by pursuing your dreams? Pay attention to what you feel and hope to achieve. Allow your passion, excitement, and "hunger" to be the driving force to your behavior. Act on your "hunger pangs."

Your life belongs to you. We've all heard the expression, "Life is what you make it." In this case, your dreams are what you take responsibility to think about, follow through with, and achieve. Your ability to reach your dreams is up to you.

Share Your Dreams With Others

"It takes a lot of courage to show your dreams to someone else." ~Erma Bombeck

Erma Bombeck also noted the importance of courage as it relates to your dreams. Bombeck espoused that you require a lot of courage to share your hopes and dreams for the future with another human being.

It might be a challenge for you to think of your own dreams because they seem too fantastic even for you to consider. So, you might be asking yourself, "How could I possibly say these things out loud? They might think I'm completely ridiculous!"

And that's where the courage comes in. Sharing your dreams with someone may require you to muster up every last bit of courage you have.

Develop the confidence to share your dreams by:

Writing down what you'll say when you talk about your dreams with someone else. Seeing your ideas and dreams on paper will help you focus on what you really want.

Practicing saying it in front of a mirror. Maybe you've never talked about your dreams. Familiarize yourself with how they'll sound by saying them a few times aloud to yourself.

Planning a time to share your thoughts. You can do this one casually so as not to overly draw attention to your desired discussion. For example, you can tell your husband something like, "Let's have a nice, quiet dinner at home this evening," to ensure you'll have the time and the relaxed atmosphere to openly talk about your hopes for the future.

Strengthening your resolve. Tell yourself the reasons why you want to share your dreams with the one you chose. Are they involved somehow in your best life plan? Next, tell yourself you can do this because you deserve to live your dreams.

Courage can get us through a lot of challenging situations. When it comes to your dreams, your courage comes into play. But when you can muster up the confidence to discuss your wildest fantasies with someone you trust, it will feel great. Plus, you'll be well on your way to actively creating your desired life.

Ask Yourself, "Why Not?"

"There are those that look at things the way they are, and ask why... I dream of things that never were, and ask why not."
~Robert Kennedy

Regardless of your politics, you've likely heard of Robert Francis Kennedy and found him to be a fascinating human being. A member of the Kennedy clan, RFK, as he's known, rose to serve as a New York senator until his death by assassination in 1968. Inspiring and positive-thinking, RFK made this statement during one of his speeches in the 1960s.

This quote really makes us think. It appears that what RFK is saying is, instead of just standing on the sidelines and questioning what everyone is doing, to envision what could be happening instead.

In this quotation, it seems that RFK is issuing a call to action to all of us.

To generate ideas that lead to your dreams:

Imagine how to resolve an issue. For example, maybe you see the place that you live as the major obstacle to pursuing your dream goal of acting. So, in the best of circumstances, where could you live to be exposed more to drama and theatre?

If you believe Hollywood is the very best place to pursue your acting goals but is impossible for you to pursue now, what is the next best place?

Maybe you live in Tennessee and work for a company in Tennessee that would allow you to transfer to work in a larger city in the state, like Nashville, which might get you more acting opportunities.

Do some homework related to your dreams. Continuing with the example of your wanting to act, you could check out Nashville to see the available opportunities there for practicing your desired craft.

During your research, maybe you discover more than 5-10 community and professional theaters there. Next, you could plan to visit Nashville to explore those venues and talk to some individuals who work there.

Brainstorm about how to take some baby steps toward your dream. For example, contact your local community theater where you live now and begin auditioning for parts as soon as possible.

Some would say that Robert Kennedy was the ultimate dreamer based on his quotation above. To visualize a way to attain an existence that you've fantasized about for a long time, consider now how to go about achieving your desired life.

You have all the reason in the world to achieve your grandest dreams. Imagination plus innovation equals realization.
Denis Waitley

« Chapter Three »

MAKE YOUR DREAM COME TRUE

"A dream doesn't become reality through magic; it takes sweat, determination and hard work." ~Colin Powell

IN THIS QUOTE, Colin Powell, a well-known politician, spoke of what he believes it takes for your dreams to come to fruition. Powell says that there's no magic that will make our dreams materialize.

Instead, he believed we have to wholly exert ourselves to make our goal happen and to keep focused on the results we want. The harder you work and the longer you stick to it, the more likely it is that your dream will become a reality.

Make your dream a reality by putting these strategies into play:

1. Avoid believing your dream could magically happen. Instead, believe in the power of you. Make the connection between your dreams and your effort. You could do this by adopting a new mantra like, "I hold the power to create what I want in my life."

2. Invest hard work to create the life you want. To illustrate, if you want to have your own business, put some work behind it by studying businesses like the one you want.

3. Interview others. Formulate a list of questions to ask those who've created a life, business, or style of living that's close to what you want. Gather as much information as possible.

4. Keep your eyes on the prize. When you know what you really want and begin expending some elbow grease to get there, it's easier to stay determined to achieve it.

5. Allot extra time toward creating the life of your dreams. For example, a couple of hours every weekend can keep you heading straight into your wildest fantasies.

Yes, to turn your hopes and wishes into reality, you'll likely be required to put in plenty of sweat equity, time, and determination. However, the life you lust after is within your reach if you're willing to do the work necessary to achieve it.

Create A Life That Truly Brings You Joy

"The most pitiful among men is he who turns his dreams into silver and gold." ~Khalil Gibran

Gibran was a poet, writer, and artist. He shared his personal philosophies about life through his many writings, including fiction, poems, and short stories.

In this quote, Gibran stresses that if one's dream is based solely on earning money, it would be unfortunate or even pitiful. Gibran is saying that going after your dreams is less about money and more about pursuing your dreams for your own satisfaction.

Although it's wonderful if you can turn the things you love to do into your life's work, it's wise to initially choose that line of work because of your love for it, rather than the dollars you can make doing it.

Follow this course of action to pursue a life you'll love:

1. Tap into your dreams to know where you're headed. Know all about them. When you truly listen to the beat of your own drum, you'll be surer of the direction you're heading.

2. Infuse activities related to your dreams into your daily life. When you tap into the content of your treasured thoughts, you'll be ready to do some activities each day that relate to them.

3. Keep your day job as you pursue your dreams. So as not to confuse achieving your dreams with your financial supports, continue with your normal work, at least until you're well-established in your dream vocation or situation.

4. Recognize there may come a time when you can actually earn dollars from your dream. However, avoid using money as the reason to keep your dream alive.

Unleash your passion for what you desire and ride its wave to the ultimate accomplishments of your dreams. Avoid rooting your dreams in the amount of money to be made. Instead, seek out your beloved fantasies to satisfy your passion so you can experience the purest joy you've ever felt.

Make Your Dream Inevitable

"So many of our dreams at first seem impossible, then, they seem improbable, and then, when we summon the will, they soon become inevitable." ~Christopher Reeve

Christopher Reeve became a quadriplegic due to a horse-riding accident in his early 40s. Even as a quadriplegic, Reeve went on to act, write books and screenplays, direct films, and become involved in activism for those with spinal-cord injuries.

Therefore, this particular quote of Reeve's carries a powerful message to all who dare to dream.

In this saying, Reeve points out that when a dream first enters your mind, it might seem ludicrous to even think it could come to pass. Later, down the road, it seems not likely that it could ever happen. Ultimately, though, if you determine by your own personal choice that you will make your dream happen, you'll see your end result is "inevitable."

Proceed with these activities to set yourself up for your dreams to come true:

Allow an outlet for your dreams. Find ways to express your dreams. Draw pictures or paint something to signify them. Take a walk each morning and use the time to think about the logistics of making your dream happen. Meditate on your dream for ten minutes in the morning.

Even if you believe your dreams are impossible, continue ahead. Rather than ceasing to think about them, charge forward and problem-solve your way around all obstacles.

Decide to pursue your dream. Make a conscious decision to begin doing small things that relate to what you want in life. You could even say out loud something like, "I am making this happen by doing everything necessary to accomplish my desired results."

Act on your ideas. For example, perhaps you think that giving to others who are less fortunate than yourself is a wonderful thing, yet you've done nothing with this thought. Maybe it's time to follow through with some of your ideas.

Set up mini-goals and celebrate when you achieve them. If one of your dreams is a month-long trip to Egypt, what could you do now to get started in that direction?

Feel free to jot down everything you'd do in advance of the trip. Perhaps now, you could read a book about Egyptian history. Then, you can research specific Egyptian landmarks you'd like to visit. Next, gather info to help you determine what your travel budget should be. Identifying several mini-goals will compel you to move forward.

Allowing your thoughts to flow wherever, whenever, and how ever they come to you is an integral part of the process of accomplishing your life goals. To achieve something, you must first dream it.

Final Thoughts

These quotations are filled with compelling philosophies that can inspire you to continue advancing toward the sparkling existence you'd like to live. Take these sayings and learn what you will. Then, apply the listed tips immediately. When your mind is open to new or unexpected information, you increase your capacity to dream bigger.

Your dreams bring golden moments, inspiration, and incredible experiences. Visualize your best life and pursue it with all your might!

"Do all you can to make your dreams come true."
~Joel Osteen

27 DREAMS **COME TRUE**

Every great dream begins with a dreamer. Always remember, you have within you the strength, the patience, and the passion to reach for the stars to change the world.
Harriet Tubman

28 STELLA FRANCES

ACT II:

EMPOWERING WORKBOOK

invite more happiness into your life through the practice of self-reflection

30 STELLA FRANCES

« Chapter Four »

SELF-EMPOWERMENT WORKBOOK
Take Action Toward Your Dream

YOU CAN EITHER READ THE guidebook in its entirety and then come back to the workbook, working through the section and refer back to the guide for more information as needed. Or if you prefer, you can read a chapter of the guide, and then work through the corresponding pages in this workbook. Either method works. Choose the one that works best for you and your style of learning.

Work through the material at your own pace. There is no right or wrong way to start making your dreams come true.

Take your time and really think about what you want in your life. It's important to write things down.

Not only will it help you get very clear about what you want, it also helps deepen your connection with it and gets you well on your way towards manifesting the things you want. It's also nice to be able to look back a few weeks or months from now and notice how much of what you've wanted to change in your life has already changed for the better.

As you read through the Guidebook in ACTI, you'll learn that you have to change your mind at a conscious and subconscious level to create something different than before.

Writing will help you get there sooner. Ideally, grab a pen, get comfortable, turn your phone off, and start working through the short exercises of this workbook. Run out of space? Use extra paper and express yourself. You don't have to work through in one sitting. Take your time, reflect on what you want to accomplish, write it down, and then come back when you're ready to work on the next section.

Let your soul be your guide.

33 DREAMS **COME TRUE**

All our dreams can come true,
if we have the courage to
pursue them.
Walt Disney

Accept the Fact that You Dream

How to focus on what you want and what you already have in order to attract more of it. Knowing what you don't want is the first step in attracting what you really want out of life.

1. What are your top 3 dreams for your life?

1_____
2_____
3_____

2. How often do you think about your dreams and life goals? Circle the response that best fits.

Daily, At Least Once	1-3 Times Weekly	1-3 Times Monthly
4 Times A Year	Once A Year	Never

3. What do you think about having and pursuing your dreams? *For example if you think that: it's silly, your dreams are unattainable, you're too old or too young, you lack time or money to pursue them, etc..., write it here.*

_____
_____
_____
_____

Plant Your Dream

4. Do you live in a location where you can easily pursue your dreams? If not, list some places where you could go after your heart's desires.

_____

_____

_____

_____

5. How is your career going? Are you doing work that interests you or makes you happy and fulfilled? If not, what are the jobs or careers you'd love to have?

_____

_____

_____

_____

Dream Your Biggest Dreams, Regardless of What Others Think

6. What are some of your own personal philosophies - the values and beliefs that are most important to you?

_____
_____
_____
_____

7. Is there someone in your life who tries to stop you from going after your dreams? If so, who? How do you respond when someone refuses to accept, acknowledge, or even makes fun of your plan for the future?

_____
_____
_____
_____

8. If you want to respond in a way that emphasizes the importance of your dreams to you, what are three things you'll do the next time someone refuses to take your dreams seriously?

_____
_____
_____
_____

A dream doesn't become reality through magic; it takes sweat, determination and hard work.
Colin Powell

Have the Courage to Pursue Your Dreams

9. Create a vision board for your dreams. What supplies will you need to do it? List them here.

_____
_____
_____
_____

10. What actions will you take to begin moving toward your desired life goals right now?

_____
_____
_____
_____

11. How will you respond if you feel afraid or unsure about pursuing your dreams? What will you do to show you have the courage to go after what you want?

_____
_____
_____
_____

Take Responsibility for Your Dreams so You'll Develop a Hunger to Achieve Them

12. How readily do you take responsibility for yourself and your life

_____
_____
_____
_____

13. What are 3 things you can do to show more responsibility for yourself?

_____
_____
_____
_____

14. When you feel an urge to do something related to a life goal, what do you do? Ignore it or step forward and pursue your next step toward achieving it?

_____
_____
_____
_____

Talk Out Loud About Your Dreams

15. Have you ever spoken about your hopes and wishes for the future with anyone? If so, who was it and how did it go? Who else can you tell about your dreams?

_____
_____
_____
_____

Imagine the Best for Your Future

16. Write your dream for the future here. Imagine what your life would be like if you go after what you want.

_____
_____
_____
_____

Have Determination, Put in Some Hard Work, and Break a Sweat

17. What can you do to show you have focus on your goals and are determined to meet them?

_____
_____
_____

18. List three "work" tasks that you can begin doing to push forward toward your dreams.

1 _____
2 _____
3 _____

Refuse to Make Your Dreams and Your Life All about the Money

19. If your worries about money keep you from pursuing your best life, write a couple of possible solutions here, such as how you can go after what you want and live a leaner life financially.

_____
_____
_____
_____

20. On the flip side, is there a possibility that you could earn some money in your quest to live your dream life? How? *Consider maintaining your full-time job for now and achieving goals "on the side" for a bit of cash until you're ready to make bigger life changes.*

_____
_____
_____
_____

Summon the Will to Achieve Your Dreams

21. What are some of the ways that you express your dreams?

_____
_____
_____
_____

22. Set 3 Mini-Goals here that will ensure you're moving toward your life goals.

1_____
2_____
3_____

43 DREAMS **COME TRUE**

To accomplish great things, we must not only act, but also dream; not only plan, but also <u>believe</u>.
Anatole France

ACT III:

KEY FACTS

46 STELLA FRANCES

« Chapter Five »

DISCOVER YOUR PASSION

How to Find Your Life's Passion

It seems that we are all in search of our life's passion, but what is a passion anyway? In short, it's the perfect fulfilling combination of career, love, family, dreams and reality.

You may feel that spending a few moments thinking about your passions and dreams is a waste of precious time – what with all the other obligations tugging at your sleeve: career, kids, bills, errands, etc.

However, these few moments might just be the defining moments of your life! You could discover the one thing that enables you to find true happiness! In fact, most of us could benefit by spending more time considering our life's passion.

Here are 8 tips to help you discover your life's passion so you can live a fulfilling life:

1. **Evaluate.** What do you feel is lacking in your life? What do you have that fulfills you? Make a list, and consider options that bring you what you lack. **Feel gratitude** and appreciation for the good things you have that fulfill you.

2. **Set goals.** Write out your most important short and long-term goals and dreams, along with a plan to achieve them. Divide your plan into small steps that you know you can accomplish. For example, if you always wanted to open a clothing store, start taking classes on business or fashion at the local college. Small, achievable steps assure your success!

3. **Don't sweat the small stuff.** Decide which of your stressors are small issues and which ones are large. Is that loud neighbor a real concern or can you let that one go? By **letting the small stressors go**, you can free up your mind to strategize ways to reduce, eliminate, or cope with what stresses you the most.

4. **Analyze your time.** Which activities take up most of your time? Do you desire more time for other, more enjoyable activities? If so, then develop a plan to restructure the time allotted for each activity. **Make a schedule** with your priorities and stick to it.

5. **Consider your fears.** What is stopping you now from taking steps towards what you want in life? Is it a fear that you won't succeed or that others will think less of you? Do you fear

how things might change if you are successful? Endeavor to fulfill your life despite fear. Facing your fears will make you feel empowered and more capable.

6. **Make a daily success plan.** Think of small changes you can implement each day to improve your life. Each day's accomplishments will show you that you are, indeed, moving toward fulfilling your life's passion!

7. **Leave regret behind.** Once you start feeling success in pursuing your life's passion, you may wish you had started earlier in your life. Push these thoughts of regret out of your mind. **To eliminate regret,** remind yourself of this wonderful opportunity you've discovered that is changing your present and future!

8. **Seek positive advice.** Talk to anyone and everyone you can think of to glean positive tips, advice, and experiences. Seek out those people that you feel have it all – everything you may be looking for in life. Find out their secrets, their perspectives, and the thoughts that motivate them.

Pursuing your life's passion can start you on a journey that brings you more joy than you have ever imagined. Following these tips and techniques will help you develop a successful strategy for turning your hopes, dreams and desires into your reality. Enjoy the journey!

All men dream, but not equally. Those who dream by night in the dusty recesses of their minds, wake in the day to find that it was vanity: but the dreamers of the day are dangerous men, for they may act on their dreams with open eyes, to make them possible.
T.E. Lawrence

Finding Your Passion Through the Power of Words

Do you feel as if you're living a passionless life?

Do you desire the same passion that you see in other people? It can be difficult to go through life without a true passion.

There are many things that can cause you to live a life without passion. It's possible that an unhappy childhood stifled your dreams, or you've never had an opportunity to develop your aspirations. Maybe indulging in your passion makes you feel guilty. Or perhaps you don't have time in your busy schedule to explore and enjoy the very things that could bring you joy.

Today, make the commitment to pursue your passion!

Give Yourself the Freedom to Discover Passion

You're a deserving person! You have the right and the need to feel passionate about the things that are near and dear to you.

You may not even realize what you're missing if you never had a chance to find and develop your goals. Discover your passion and embrace it because it can lead you to a life without limits. You can turn your passion into a career, hobby, or a way to network with people.

Passion can improve every aspect of your life. It's your passion that makes your life positive and fulfilling.

When first starting your quest toward your dreams, you may wonder, "What is there to be passionate about?" That's perfectly normal. Many people start out with the same question.

Even if you feel that way, it's never too late for you to find something that fills you with an inner joy and peace. Your life begins anew when you pursue your dreams, desires, and goals.

You can gain a fresh perspective in your life when you take some time to expand your comfort zone and pursue the things that you'd never considered before. For example, if you travelled to a foreign place and met new people, you would see and experience things a whole new world that will open your eyes and mind. When you do this, you may find something that's been missing from your life.

Passion Affirmations Can Spark Your Passion

You may find your passions through the power of affirmations. When you give yourself permission to be passionate, you may suddenly find that you're more enthusiastic about things than you previously dreaded.

Passion affirmations are positive statements that change the way you think about life and the world around you.

Affirmations positively influence your subconscious mind. Passion affirmations can bring to light a wonderful new way of living that's full of joy, abundance, and gratitude.

For example, when you get out of bed each morning, you might say to yourself, *"Igniting my passion is another way of revealing how much I love myself."*

Every time you repeat this statement, you're reaffirming that new positive thought in your mind. At the same time, you're eliminating any negative thoughts that may be holding you back.

Choose affirmations that you feel speak to you and relate to your own feelings. Repeat them several times each day and soon you'll discover the joys of living a passionate life.

Nothing happens unless first we dream.
Carl Sandburg

WHAT ARE YOUR SECRET TALENTS?

What Talents Are Hiding Within You?

Many people have grown up believing they didn't have anything special or unique to add to the world. Perhaps they came from challenging surroundings or had no encouragement for their gifts, so they went unrecognized. Or maybe they repressed their talents because they felt ashamed. Whatever the reason, it's all too easy to believe our talents and passions are not worth pursuing.

Everyone Has Talent!

A great many of us are wandering around with the belief that we aren't all that interesting when it comes to our natural gifts. But we all have more talent than we think we do.

Very often we hear news stories about children with incredible abilities. Many of them are entertainers or child prodigies featured on daytime talk shows. While it's incredible to see these talented young children, don't forget about your own children's talents, which might not be as obvious. They may not be as advanced as the kids on television, but everyone's talents are worth developing.

Children are often inspired after watching the Olympics and parents rush out to enroll the kids in gymnastics or swimming programs. They might possibly be the next Michael Phelps or they may never make it to the Olympics, but they will learn a new skill, get exercise, and meet new friends.

Adults may be inspired by their favorite sports hero. If you daydream about winning the Tour de France, then start small by joining a local cycling club.

Be Realistic

We shouldn't delude ourselves and believe we can do all things. We need to be realistic about what we can accomplish but that doesn't mean we shouldn't try new things or take classes to learn something new.

If you've always wanted to be a Broadway actor, audition for a local community theater group. Many people can fulfill their passion on a smaller, local level.

You might decorate beautiful children's birthday cakes, but should you attempt to decorate your niece's wedding cake? Be realistic about your skills and how much time it will take but feel free to take some extra classes or find a mentor in the field who can help you.

Using Our Talents In Our Work

Many of us take jobs we don't like and live lives we wish were a lot more exciting or fulfilling. Instead of being discouraged with our life choices, we need to choose what we wish to do in the life we have and let our instincts lead us to our passions.

Think about what you love to do the most with regards to your job:

Maybe you love writing up detailed reports and therefore have a knack for the written word.

Maybe you get compliments on your good communications with clients. This might indicate you would be great as a public speaker or trainer.

What Do You Like?

If you still think you don't have much talent, start looking at what you love to do with your time.

- Maybe you love to sing along to your favorite song and your family and friends consistently tell you how good you are.

- Maybe you love to dance and whenever others see you they remark about your incredible agility.

- Maybe you find yourself doodling a masterpiece when you have some idle time.

If you think about what you really enjoy doing, you'll find that you've been drawn to it over the course of many months or years. It tends to be true that the better we are at something, the more we enjoy doing it.

If this doesn't ring any bells for you, think about what your favorite classes were in school. Once again, remember that we tend to love the things we're good at. Thinking about these things is an excellent way to uncover your hidden talents.

Discovering these talents is a wonderful way to find a new hobby or boost your self-esteem. If you let yourself accept that you probably have undiscovered talents, enjoy this adventure of discovery. It could very well take your life to higher levels of wealth and fulfillment.

TOP 10 INSPIRATIONAL SAYINGS

We all have those moments when we need inspiration to gain confidence and build momentum. That's why inspirational sayings are so popular.

When you live a life without inspiration, it can be a life without any real joy or passion. In those moments where you need a little pick me up or a reminder of the many great things you have in your life, you can turn to the power of inspirational words. You need to have a collection of inspirational sayings in your toolkit that resonate with you so you can get more done and still feel great.

The Top 10 Ten Inspirational Sayings You Can Use Everywhere

There are a lot of great motivational sayings out there that we can turn to when we are feeling down, but we should be using them all the time, rain or shine. Strive to incorporate inspirational sayings into your everyday life, using them to inspire you to reach higher and push harder so you can achieve all the things you have set out to do and more.

Some wonderful inspirational sayings include:

1. There is a beautiful light at the end of my tunnel.
2. I take small steps in life and value my time.
3. In order to share happiness with others, I must also be happy.
4. As I let go of dissatisfaction, I feel happiness in my life.

5. My life is full of purpose, exciting change, and many recognized deeds.

6. No matter the challenge, I will see it through.

7. I am becoming more focused and confident every day.

8. I welcome positive energy and I use that feeling to accomplish more.

9. My life is already filled with success.

10. I keep only two mental snapshots of myself: where I am and where I want to be in life.

These are all very simple inspirational sayings that work to affirm positive thoughts and attitudes in your mind. Affirmations are simply positive statements that remind you of your goals and positive uniqueness so you can boost your self-confidence.

Accomplish More with the Power of Inspirational Thinking

Inspirational sayings and affirmations can help us move forward in life and accomplish greater things than we could have ever imagined. After all, we can't deny the power of a can-do attitude. If more of us incorporate inspiration into our lives, we would all be happier and more successful people. When you incorporate positive sayings into your life, you'll find that you'll respond on a subconscious level and you'll no longer need to look very far for inspiration.

If you're down or lacking confidence, you can use inspirational sayings to find the courage to move forward and force out any negative thoughts that may be cycling through your mind. When you say these statements with gusto, you are re-affirming positive thoughts in your mind, making them a part of who you are.

Remember to use these sayings at any and every occasion to give you the inspiration you need to get through any challenge, both big and small.

NOTES AT A GLANCE

bite size, useful practical information you can put to work for you right-away.

NOTES AT A GLANCE:
Dreams Come True: 1-2-3

1. BE OPEN TO YOUR DREAM

- ✓ Choose Your Dream
- ✓ Nix the Naysayers

2. FOLLOW YOUR DREAM

- ✓ Leave Fear Behind and Go After Your Dreams
- ✓ Take 100% Responsibility in Bringing Your Dreams to Life
- ✓ Share Your Dreams With Others
- ✓ Ask Yourself, "Why Not?"

3. MAKE YOUR DREAM COME TRUE

- ✓ Leave Fear Behind and Go After Your Dream
- ✓ Take Action Toward Your Dream
- ✓ Create A Life That Truly Brings You Joy
- ✓ Make Your Dream Inevitable

NOTES AT A GLANCE:
Dreams Come True

DISCOVER YOUR PASSION
How to Find Your Life's Passion

- ✓ Evaluate
- ✓ Set goals
- ✓ Don't sweat the small stuff
- ✓ Analyze your time
- ✓ Consider your fears
- ✓ Make a daily success plan
- ✓ Leave regret behind
- ✓ Seek positive advice

Dreams are illustrations...
from the book your soul is
writing about you.
Marsha Norman

Read Much About the Subject

There are many resources on the subject. I encourage you to start learning and answering all the questions you will have after reading this simple introduction to such a complex matter.

Also, check out the short list of books I am including in the Acquiring Knowledge, section at the end of the book and other Stella Note titles that can further help you understand essential elements that contribute to our happiness and ultimately success.

66 STELLA FRANCES

ACT IV:

HAPPINESS BUILDERS

TOOLS-TO-USE

« Chapter Six »

DREAMS COME TRUE
By Katie Coluccio

It is now being called the party of the century. Last Saturday night on one of the most beautiful nights in New York City in the past year, the party at the rooftop bar of the Soho House was a celebration of the expansion of Katie Coluccio's company, Light, Love, Laugh.

The party celebrated a record-breaking 5-year success story and a world-wide presence boasting a center on every continent and one in almost every country. This company is one of the very few to become a multi-billion-dollar company within the first five years.

When asked about the company's success, it's founder and CEO, Reiki Master Katie Coluccio had this to say: "I dreamed big and I set my goals. My mission is to heal the people who will heal the planet. I believe that we can do this through all means available to us. Every kind of medicine has its place and I plan to make them available to everyone."

Light, Love, Laugh has implemented a successful model of health care centers which has allowed for the philanthropic outreach into the communities and charities that are in need. Katie has donated countless hours and money to help animals, and to clean our waterways and oceans.

She and Light, Love, Laugh have been recognized by numerous organizations for the various donations to these and other charities.

One of Katie's employees, Claudia Brown had this to say about Katie, "I love working for Katie and for this company. She values her employees and even though the company has now become world-wide, she still sees each of her employees as a person. Other companies I have worked for, you are nothing but a number."

Celebrating a presence throughout the world before the end of 5 years is an accomplishment that Katie is very proud of. She told this reporter, "I am excited to say that after reaching this milestone we can open even more community centers where those who might not be able to afford care can be seen. My goal is to bring healthcare to everyone, everywhere."

The guest list for the party ranged from employees to administrators to celebrity guests. In attendance was Stella

Frances, world-renowned spiritual life coach and rumored to be one of Katie's best friends. Zetta Karmas, another one of Katie's best friends and famous artist, was also at the party. Eddie Vedder, lead singer of Pearl Jam, was also in attendance. Mr. Vedder was seen dancing into the night with Katie and laughing the night away.

Eddie Vedder was quoted, "I believe in what Katie is doing and her vision. I feel that helping people heal is the first step to healing the planet. We all know that the planet needs healing."

Stella Frances told us, "Working with Katie throughout the past 6 years, I have seen her grow in ways that are indescribable. She has truly come to realize her vision and actualize her potential!"

Another of Katie's longtime friends, Zetta Karmas, had this to say, "Katie is an amazing example of what you can do when you put your mind to something. She has one of the most thoughtful and caring presences I have ever experienced. She has become one of my closest and best friends."

The above is an example of one of the exercises we do in my classes to help solidify a vision by seeing it in the future with our mind's eye. It was written as if it was a newspaper or magazine article about a milestone event of a successful business.

Words Of Wisdom

wise words spoken by some of the most powerful and advanced thinkers in our world.
listen to the echo of their voices and use their wisdom in your moment-to-moment life

WORDS OF WISDOM

There is only one thing that makes a dream impossible to achieve: the fear of failure.
Paulo Coelho

WORDS OF WISDOM

When you have a dream that you can't let go
of, trust your instincts and pursue it.
But remember: Real dreams take work,
They take patience, and sometimes
they require you to dig down very deep.
Be sure you're willing to do that.
Harvey Mackay

WORDS OF WISDOM

Throw your dreams into space like a kite,
and you do not know
what it will bring back,
a new life, a new friend,
a new love, a new country.
Anais Nin

Pearls Of Kindness

heartfelt affirmations for you to thrive on your path to happiness

POWERFUL HEARTFELT AFFIRMATIONS
I Am Motivated To See My Dreams Come True.

My dreams are always strongly present in my mind. *I know where I am headed and I have what it takes to get there.*

Sometimes what it takes is a little get-up-and-go! But I know that *I have all the motivation I need to see my dreams come true.*

Focus is a big part of what enables me to achieve my dreams. In order to refocus when I get distracted, I manifest patience, determination, and most of all, motivation. I know that it is through sustained work that I progress toward my dreams.

I am unwavering in my desire to manifest my dreams. Each day, I take time to reprioritize my time and other resources around my highest aspirations.

This helps me stay focused and motivated.

POWERFUL HEARTFELT AFFIRMATIONS
I Am Confident About What I Have To Offer The World.

My gifts are many, and I share them freely. And each time I do this, I am well-received. *People value what I have to give and I know it is of great worth.*

I have skills and talents that other people value. I certainly value them.

Whether I am good at cooking, fixing things, or lending a compassionate ear, *I know that my talents were given to me for the good of the world as well as for me.*

If I ever feel doubtful that I can make a difference in someone's life with what I have to offer, I remember that I have these gifts for a reason.

Today, I trust that my actions leave the legacy I want for myself. *I know that I am naturally capable of contributing to other people's lives.* And I am confident about what I have to offer the world.

RELAXING MANDALAS

EXPRESS YOUR INNER-ARTIST

beautiful mandalas to help you find inner peace by being in the moment.

You can use color pencils or just your regular pen, markers are not recommended as the ink may bleed through the paper.

RELAXING MANDALAS

Whether you're feeling overwhelmed, scattered, or just plain stressed, coloring offers a peaceful and therapeutic way to refocus and reinvigorate your mind.

This form of meditation is becoming increasingly popular as we realize stress isn't something we can just "power through". Meditative practices soothe mind chatter, allowing our inner voice to shine through.

The ritual of mandala coloring moves us into a contemplative state, encouraging us to slow down. Allow your stress to melt away as you enter the world of circles and patterns.

The word Mandala (pronunciation mon- dah- lah) means "circle" and represents the universe in Indian religions. The mandala encompasses friends, family, and communities.

The mandala teaches us life is circular. Life is never-ending. Each moment is another colorful thread in the continually growing tapestry of the universe.

Become one with the Universe as you lose yourself to the flow of lines and color. Allow yourself to move from the doing to the being as you enjoy the process of transformative ritual!

RELAXING MANDALAS

RELAXING MANDALAS

83 DREAMS **COME TRUE**

RELAXING MANDALAS

84 STELLA FRANCES

IN CLOSING

Bonus Material

a gift for you

I Am Creating The Life Of My Dreams

I am so excited about the direction my life is taking. Each day, I feel closer and closer to reaching my dreams.

I look at my progress and feel a sense of excitement and anticipation. My creative powers are growing stronger every day.

Occasionally things happen that temporarily challenge my resolve, but I am able to quickly get back on track and focus on my goals. I review my goals daily and visualize myself being successful. It feels amazing to experience that kind of success.

My progress toward my goals is rapid and effortless.

I notice that as I focus on my achieving my goals, I feel happier and more content. My friends and family are also positively impacted by my focus. It is amazing how my happiness positively affects those around me.

At night, I lie in bed and give thanks for all that I have and all that I am achieving. I am very lucky to be so blessed to have so many things in my favor. I smile inwardly and sleep soundly and peacefully every night.

In the morning, I am always eager to pursue the life of my dreams with great enthusiasm. My friends wonder how I successfully create so many positive changes in myself and in my life.

Today, I am taking a significant step toward creating the life of my dreams. My enthusiasm and courage build each day. I know the life of my dreams is right around the corner.

Self-Reflection Questions:

1. *How can I create the life of my dreams more quickly?*

2. *What is the greatest obstacle in my way right now? How can I overcome it?*

3. *What has been my greatest recent success?*

Voice your thoughts here…

_____
_____
_____
_____
_____
_____
_____
_____
_____
_____

In The Sea Of Love Find Your Happy

One word that describes me:

Outside the box...

_____

AFTERWORD

resource guide for living a better, happier purpose-driven life

A Note From Stella Frances

If you've made it this far, then I can tell we are going to be friends. You - like me - are always exploring how you can grow and be your best-self. I'm inspired by people like you and would love to embrace you as part of the tribe.

To learn more about how to *"Find Your Happy"* by creating a meaningful and purpose driven life visit StellaFrances.com or come to a private workshop or mini-retreat where we can meet in person and we can dig into Careers & Relationships over soulful conversations. For a list of upcoming events remember to go to: StellaFrances.com/events/

I'd love to connect with you and hear about your journey. So be sure to stay in touch. Feel free to send me a quick note or say hello on Facebook and keep me posted. I'm here to help.

Here's to leading a life of purpose and living with passion.

Stella xo

PS Visit the blog StellaFrances.com/blog page for daily inspiration and tips on creating the life you love living. I can help you succeed in your pursuit of happiness.

PPS As, Zig Ziglar once said... *"People often say that motivation doesn't last. Well, neither does bathing, that's why we recommend it daily"*

A SPECIAL INVITATION
Find Your Happy Discovery Call

Set up An Exclusive Appointment with A Whole New Level Of Happiness.

Are you ready to move your happiness up to a new level?

Explore and Discover What Really Matters To You. I invite you to a complimentary call with me to explore and discover the ways to bring more happiness into your life.

We all experience the ups and downs of life and I'm here to help keep you going in the right direction, just because we all deserve to be happy.

A "Find-Your-Happy" Discovery Session is a 30-minute call. where we talk about where in life you are now and where you'd love to be.

Specifically, here's what we will cover during our call:

<u>The 3 D's:</u>

1. *Discover* the longing and discontent in the areas of your life you'd like to improve and what is costing you to stay where you are. That would be our first step.

2. *Design* a clear vision for the quality of life you desire and what's worth to take happiness to the next level. That would be our second step.

3. ***Decide*** to take today the action that will move you from where you are to where you want to be. That would be the third step in taking your Happiness to a higher level.

Leave this session feeling uplifted and inspired knowing that you have the power to change your life and that the power within you is far greater than your current life conditions and circumstances.

Right now, you're standing at the doorway to your new ideal life. Get clear on exactly where you are, what you'd like to create, and the next most important step you can take that will move you in the direction of a happier-purpose driven life.

Join me for a complimentary 30-min. discovery call. Every week I make sure I carve out a chunk of time to offer free service to community. This is my way to say thank you and "pay-it-forward." As you can imaging spots are limited. To schedule your session, jump over to the website and let's talk soon. To access my calendar, go to StellaFrances.com/calendar/

I'm here to help.

YOUR NEXT BEST STEP
Need More In-Depth Guidance Creating A Happiness Based Life?

These will help...

We have created some incredibly in-depth programs, courses and products to help you every step of the way on your pursuit of happiness. And as with everything we do at Elevated Awareness, they come with a 100% results-backed guarantee. That's just how confident I am they work.

Two great places to start are:

An Empowering Self-Discovery Adventure

Find Your Happy

Find it and Claim it. Know who you are and be who you are. With this step-by-step framework Stella helps her clients take time to find themselves, understand what they want in their lives, and take effective right action to make their dreams come true. This program is for you if you want to bring more happiness and success into your life by finding meaning, purpose and direction.

Happiness fuels success; **if you want to be more successful, be happier.** Stella's coaching will empower you to achieve your goals whilst simultaneously increasing your happiness. Take action and begin your pursuit of true happiness, today.

A Journey Into Life Mastery
THE PASSPORT

Passport to your dream. If you are ready for a new destination. If it feels like something is missing where you are in your life right now, get ready to DEFINE your IDEAL outcome and DECIDE to go after it.

If you're willing to commit to your happiness and ready to take action to change your life, then you have found the program that will help you move forward.

THE PASSPORT is a step-by-step proven system that helps you get crystal clear on what you want and gives you the tools and strategies to stay true to yourself. Learn the simple steps that will take you from wherever you are now (stuck, frustrated, scared, unhappy) to confident and fulfilled as you learn exactly how to define your dream and develop a concrete plan to achieve it.

When you are in harmony with your soul's purpose and with what you are here to be and do, things get easier. This is the most passionate, wondrous way to live life. Sign up and start living the life you were meant to live.

VIP Day Every intensive is unique. You may choose to come work with me in person, or virtually from the comfort of your own home or office. Join me for jam-packed self-discovery action over the course of a fun filled day.

STELLA NOTES & CLUB ★ HAPPY

Solutions From The Soul

Winning ways to play the game of life. Check out this popular mini guide series on finding true lasting happiness and take your life to the next level. Stella Notes are short writings super loaded with practical tools, easy-to-use strategies, and pearls of wisdom to help you uncover your passions, remove roadblocks and get you moving from where you are to where you want to be.

Imagine what it would feel like to belong to a group that combined the benefits of a social group, mastermind group, support group, cheerleader group. Imagine what it would feel like to create relationships with like-minded people who not only understand your thirst to discover your truth and make your dreams come true, but who also believe that you can achieve the goals you set for yourself.

These are just some of the benefits you will enjoy as a member of Club-Happy. Visit StellaFrances.com/clubhappy

Curious to know more? All of the courses, products and free resources to support you on your life journey can be found at: StellaFrances.com

Make your journey a fun one.

"Success Begins with Happiness"
Stella Frances

ABOUT STELLA FRANCES

Mentor, Coach, Speaker, Creator of Stella-Notes

Stella Frances, founder of Elevated Awareness, inspires and empowers all those that are drawn to her to live their highest vision in the context of love and joy.

As a Success Principles, Jack Canfield Certified Trainer and as a Mary Morrissey Certified DreamBuilder Coach, Stella can help you design and manifest a life that's in harmony with your soul's purpose.

After 15 successful years in the I.T. industry, Stella-Frances found herself more passionate in coaching her clients around systems for life than in I.T. systems. Her passion is teaching clients discover & unlock their unique potential, find true happiness and achieve success to live a life they LOVE living.

Stella is an inspiring speaker, passionate educator, and a highly sought-after happiness coach.

What is the biggest challenge you're facing right now? And what would you love to create? Let Stella help you, or your employees break through the obstacles that are holding you back. You will be glad you did.

To contact Stella, go to her website at StellaFrances.com

Qualifications and Certifications
- Success Principles Trainer - Jack Canfield (Chicken Soup for the Soul)
- DreamBuilder Coach - Mary Morrissey, Transformational Coaching
- Access Bars™ Practitioner Gary Douglas, Access Consciousness
- Langevin Certified Instructor/Facilitator

PROGRAMS AND WORKSHOPS

Stella Frances gives talks and leads workshops all over the United States and the Caribbean Islands.

She also conducts retreats, intensives, and training programs.

To learn more, go to StellaFrances.Com/Events

Island Retreat with Stella Frances
The Voyage
ADVENTURES INTO HAPPINESS

The ticket to happiness is hidden in your heart. Get out of your day-to-day grind and jump into the source of true happiness. Connect with nature as you set your intentions to bring more happiness into your life.

Create a powerful vision of your IDEAL life, set goals and define effective action to make it happen. Learn how to change your thoughts to change your world.

If you'd like Stella's personal help in defining the framework and start building an exciting life based on your definition of happiness, these small-group private retreats held in exclusive locations like the quaint Bahamas, Jamaica, and Jupiter Beach offer a tranquil, transformational environment and personalized support you need to awaken to the best <u>You</u>.

Reject stress and give yourself the gift of time to attain inner-peace and a sense of empowerment. Get inspired with our sunrise meditation on the beach. Enjoy healthy delicious freshly cooked meals. Come home with an island mindset and a solid plan to maintain it, no matter how gray the sky gets.

Recharge and Reboot At A Retreat By-The-Sea.

For information and to reserve your spot, contact Stella at Happier@StellaFrances.com

Bring The Power Of Change To Your Organization

Steps to Success

KEYNOTE, WORKSHOP, AND TRAINING

Positive change and profound success are the results when your employees and managers, experience **Steps to Success** in a live group workshop, training, or keynote.

Not only will your team be inspired and motivated to achieve greater success, but they'll also learn how to up-level all their mind-sets, actions, relationships, and strategic alliances.

Steps to Success Keynote, Workshop, or Training will empower them with strategies that make them more productive, help put more money in their paychecks, help them function better within their workgroups, and respond more effectively and productively to everyday events.

The **Steps to Success** *is ideal for groups such as:*
- ❖ Small-business owners
- ❖ Managers and executives
- ❖ Corporate workgroups and new hires
- ❖ Professional practitioners and their staffs
- ❖ Work-at-home employees and telecommuters
- ❖ Employees facing layoff or transfer

To learn more, go to StellaFrances.com or contact Stella at Happier@StellaFrances.com

90-Day Programs with Stella Frances

The Passport
Voyage into Happiness

A Life Mastery Course of Action. Getting you from where you are to where you want to be.

Find *Your* Happy
A Self-Discovery & Empowerment Journey

Bring more happiness into your life by finding meaning, purpose and direction.

The Ticket
You Were Born To Be Happy

A 2-STEP FORMULA TO BRING MORE HAPPINESS & SUCCESS INTO YOUR PROFESSIONAL LIFE

Step 1: Making your business more effective.

Step 2: Becoming a more effective *you.*

The Dream Builder
Journey into The Spirit
The Spiritual Laws of Success

Learn how everything is created twice – and how you can use that truth to build your dreams effortlessly.

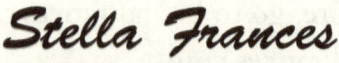

YOUR HAPPINESS COACH
GROUP. ONE-ON-ONE. VIP-DAY. RETREATS. WORKSHOPS

101 DREAMS **COME TRUE**

Weekend Workshops with Stella Frances

THE MECHANICS OF LIFE

Elevating Self-Awareness

An Irresistibly Fun Series Of
5 Self-Growth Mix-&-Match Workshops

#1. Master the Mindset of Success.
#2. Goal Setting For Growth.
#3. Building Inner Confidence.
#4. The Power Of Saying No.
#5.: Elevate Your Energy.

The Vision
Tailor Life to Your Dreams

Start actively pursuing the dream that will give you the joy, confidence and happiness you're longing for.

To learn more, go to StellaFrances.com or contact Stella at Happier@StellaFrances.com

Stella Frances
YOUR HAPPINESS COACH
GROUP. ONE-ON-ONE. VIP-DAY. RETREATS. WORKSHOPS

Aquiring Knowledge And Additional Resources For Happiness And Success

I trust you enjoyed reading this Stella Notes book and have found it both helpful and interesting. Above all I hope it piqued your curiosity enough to make you want to dive deeper and learn more.

I suggest and recommend that you read something educational and motivational every day, at least 15-minutes a day, or more. Create a new ritual to inspire and motivate yourself.

Keep reading, keep learning, and keep practicing as you work your way towards the life of your dreams. Happiness is attainable by each one of us. Make it happen.

Knowledge is Power

Also Available In The Stella Notes Series

- ✓ Law of Attraction
- ✓ Imagine
- ✓ Dreams Come True
- ✓ Being Happier
- ✓ Inspired
- ✓ No Worries
- ✓ Happy by Habit
- ✓ Mindfully Yours
- ✓ Stuck No More
- ✓ Love ThySelf

Take Your Happiness To The Next Level... Download The FREE Happiness Tools

At StellaFrances.com/resources

Tool #1: Daily Gratitude Journal

Use the Gratitude Journal to record you wins and gifts of the day. It's an awesome self-discovery tool that can help you connect with your unique character strengths.

Tool #2: Stuck? Unstick Yourself Now Worksheet

An easy tool to use for when you feel stuck or want to generate new ideas for a project or goal. This super-effective brainstorming tool helps you come up with lots of new ideas and choose 3 actions to move forward with.

Tool #3: Stressed? Overwhelmed? Speedy Priority Finder

Sometimes your day-to-day priorities differ from your life's priorities. Use this tool to feel more in control and less overwhelmed. Clarify a path to set and realize top priorities.

Tool #4: Daily Success Habits Exercise

By making small changes to your daily routine you can make BIG changes in your life and career. Define 5 new success habits, to help you be more effective.

5-DAY SELF-DISCOVERY COURSE

In this powerful FREE **Grow-Expand-Thrive** mini course -delivered to your email address- you will learn winning ways to find your happy and start living a more fulfilled and meaningful life. Register today at StellaFrances.com

www.ingramcontent.com/pod-product-compliance
Lightning Source LLC
Chambersburg PA
CBHW022106160426
43198CB00008B/375